The Ultimate
HUNTING
Journal

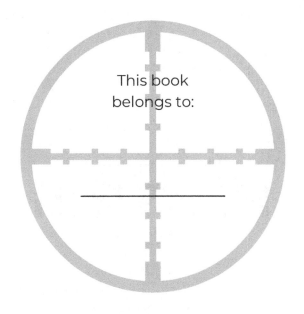

This book
belongs to:

_____

Dates: _____

Journals by North of the Present
Leslie McConnell

The Ultimate
HUNTING
Journal

How to use this hunt tracker...

This journal provides space to track 45 hunts.

It is broken down into three sections.

The first section allows you to detail the specifics of each hunt. Track things like date and time, weather, firearm, game hunted, wildlife observed, and even the phase of the moon! The first two pages show an example.

The second section provides space for you to total your hunts for each month.

The third section provides space to track your hunting-related purchases and expenses.

Begin this journal at any time of the year! Keep your journals to look at trends over time, for historical reference, or for preserving memories with family and friends.

Nov. 28, 2021
Date

6:30am / 11:00am
Start/End Time

Your GPS coordinates or favorite tree stand!
Location

Weather

6mph, gusty
Wind Speed

Wind Direction

Shade the moon based on the phase.

Moon

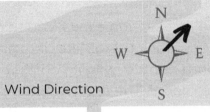

38°
Temperature

Whitetail bucks
What are you hunting today?

Dad's rifle

Firearm/Gear

Went solo today

Hunting Companions

What did you see today?

Circle what you saw OR write the number observed on top of the image.

Spied a nice 8-point, but he was too far away
for a good shot. Next time...

What did you harvest?

Field Notes

Saw a good scrape about 50 yards north from

the tree stand.

Remember to bring more snacks next time.

Date

Start/End Time

Location

Weather

Wind Speed

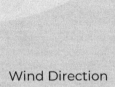

Wind Direction

Shade the moon based on the phase.

Moon

Temperature

What are you hunting today?

Firearm/Gear

Hunting Companions

What did you see today?

Circle what you saw OR write the number observed on top of the image.

What did you harvest?

Field Notes

_____

_____

_____

_____

_____

Date

Start/End Time

Location

Weather

Wind Speed

Wind Direction

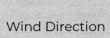

Shade the moon based on the phase.

Moon

Temperature

What are you hunting today?

Firearm/Gear

Hunting Companions

What did you see today?

Circle what you saw OR write the number observed on top of the image.

What did you harvest?

Field Notes

_____

_____

_____

_____

_____

Date

Start/End Time

Location

Weather

Wind Speed

Wind Direction

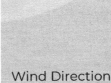

Shade the moon based on the phase.

Moon

Temperature

What are you hunting today?

Firearm/Gear

Hunting Companions

What did you see today?
Circle what you saw OR write the number observed on top of the image.

What did you harvest?

Field Notes

_____

_____

_____

_____

_____

Date

Start/End Time

Location

Weather

Wind Speed

N

W ← → E

S

Wind Direction

Shade the moon based on the phase.

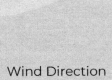

Moon

Temperature

What are you hunting today?

Firearm/Gear

Hunting Companions

What did you see today?
Circle what you saw OR write the number observed on top of the image.

What did you harvest?

Field Notes

_____

_____

_____

_____

_____

Date

Start/End Time

Location

Weather

Wind Speed

Wind Direction

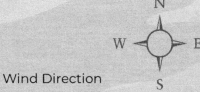

Shade the moon based on the phase.

Moon

Temperature

What are you hunting today?

Firearm/Gear

Hunting Companions

What did you see today?

Circle what you saw OR write the number observed on top of the image.

What did you harvest?

Field Notes

_____

_____

_____

_____

_____

Date

Start/End Time

Location

Weather

Wind Speed

Wind Direction

Shade the moon based on the phase.

Moon

Temperature

What are you hunting today?

Firearm/Gear

Hunting Companions

What did you see today?

Circle what you saw OR write the number observed on top of the image.

What did you harvest?

Field Notes

_____

_____

_____

_____

_____

Date

Start/End Time

Location

Weather

Wind Speed

Wind Direction

Shade the moon based on the phase.

Moon

Temperature

What are you hunting today?

Firearm/Gear

Hunting Companions

What did you see today?
Circle what you saw OR write the number observed on top of the image.

What did you harvest?

Field Notes

_____

_____

_____

_____

_____

Date

Start/End Time

Location

Weather

Wind Speed

Wind Direction

Shade the moon based on the phase.

Moon

Temperature

What are you hunting today?

Firearm/Gear

Hunting Companions

What did you see today?
Circle what you saw OR write the number observed on top of the image.

What did you harvest?

Field Notes

_____

_____

_____

_____

_____

Date

Start/End Time

Location

Weather

Wind Speed

Wind Direction

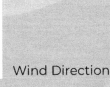

Shade the moon based on the phase.

Moon

Temperature

What are you hunting today?

Firearm/Gear

Hunting Companions

What did you see today?
Circle what you saw OR write the number observed on top of the image.

What did you harvest?

Field Notes

_____

_____

_____

_____

_____

Date

Start/End Time

Location

Weather

Wind Speed

Wind Direction

Shade the moon based on the phase.

Moon

Temperature

What are you hunting today?

Firearm/Gear

Hunting Companions

What did you see today?

Circle what you saw OR write the number observed on top of the image.

What did you harvest?

Field Notes

_____

_____

_____

_____

_____

Date

Start/End Time

Location

Weather

Wind Speed

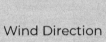

Wind Direction

Shade the moon based on the phase.

Moon

Temperature

What are you hunting today?

Firearm/Gear

Hunting Companions

What did you see today?

Circle what you saw OR write the number observed on top of the image.

What did you harvest?

Field Notes

_____

_____

_____

_____

_____

Date

Start/End Time

Location

Weather

Wind Speed

Wind Direction

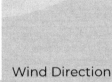

Shade the moon based on the phase.

Moon

Temperature

What are you hunting today?

Firearm/Gear

Hunting Companions

What did you see today?
Circle what you saw OR write the number observed on top of the image.

What did you harvest?

Field Notes

_____

_____

_____

_____

_____

Date

Start/End Time

Location

Weather

Wind Speed

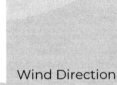

Wind Direction

Shade the moon based on the phase.

Moon

Temperature

What are you hunting today?

Firearm/Gear

Hunting Companions

What did you see today?

Circle what you saw OR write the number observed on top of the image.

What did you harvest?

Field Notes

_____

_____

_____

_____

_____

Date

Start/End Time

Location

Weather

Wind Speed

Wind Direction

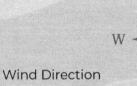

*Shade the moon
based on the phase.*

Moon

Temperature

What are you hunting today?

Firearm/Gear

Hunting Companions

What did you see today?

Circle what you saw OR write the number observed on top of the image.

What did you harvest?

Field Notes

_____

_____

_____

_____

_____

Date

Start/End Time

Location

Weather

Wind Speed

Wind Direction

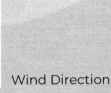

Shade the moon based on the phase.

Moon

Temperature

What are you hunting today?

Firearm/Gear

Hunting Companions

What did you see today?
Circle what you saw OR write the number observed on top of the image.

What did you harvest?

Field Notes

_____

_____

_____

_____

_____

Date

Start/End Time

Location

Weather

Wind Speed

Wind Direction

Shade the moon based on the phase.

Moon

Temperature

What are you hunting today?

Firearm/Gear

Hunting Companions

What did you see today?

Circle what you saw OR write the number observed on top of the image.

What did you harvest?

Field Notes

_____

_____

_____

_____

_____

Date

Start/End Time

Location

Weather

Wind Speed

Wind Direction

Shade the moon based on the phase.

Moon

Temperature

What are you hunting today?

Firearm/Gear

Hunting Companions

What did you see today?

Circle what you saw OR write the number observed on top of the image.

What did you harvest?

Field Notes

_____

_____

_____

_____

_____

Date

Start/End Time

Location

Weather

Wind Speed

Wind Direction

Shade the moon based on the phase.

Moon

Temperature

What are you hunting today?

Firearm/Gear

Hunting Companions

What did you see today?

Circle what you saw OR write the number observed on top of the image.

What did you harvest?

Field Notes

_____

_____

_____

_____

_____

Date

Start/End Time

Location

Weather

Wind Speed

Wind Direction

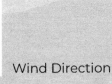

Shade the moon based on the phase.

Moon

Temperature

What are you hunting today?

Firearm/Gear

Hunting Companions

What did you see today?

Circle what you saw OR write the number observed on top of the image.

What did you harvest?

Field Notes

_____

_____

_____

_____

_____

Date

Start/End Time

Location

Weather

Wind Speed

Wind Direction

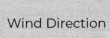

Shade the moon based on the phase.

Moon

Temperature

What are you hunting today?

Firearm/Gear

Hunting Companions

What did you see today?
Circle what you saw OR write the number observed on top of the image.

What did you harvest?

Field Notes

_____

_____

_____

_____

_____

Date

Start/End Time

Location

Weather

Wind Speed

Wind Direction

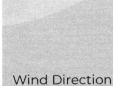

Shade the moon based on the phase.

Moon

Temperature

What are you hunting today?

Firearm/Gear

Hunting Companions

What did you see today?

Circle what you saw OR write the number observed on top of the image.

What did you harvest?

Field Notes

_____

_____

_____

_____

_____

Date

Start/End Time

Location

Weather

Wind Speed

Wind Direction

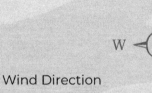

Shade the moon based on the phase.

Moon

Temperature

What are you hunting today?

Firearm/Gear

Hunting Companions

What did you see today?
Circle what you saw OR write the number observed on top of the image.

What did you harvest?

Field Notes

_____

_____

_____

_____

_____

Date

Start/End Time

Location

Weather

Wind Speed

Wind Direction

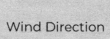

Shade the moon based on the phase.

Moon

Temperature

What are you hunting today?

Firearm/Gear

Hunting Companions

What did you see today?

Circle what you saw OR write the number observed on top of the image.

What did you harvest?

Field Notes

_____

_____

_____

_____

_____

Date

Start/End Time

Location

Weather

Wind Speed

Wind Direction

Shade the moon based on the phase.

Moon

Temperature

What are you hunting today?

Firearm/Gear

Hunting Companions

What did you see today?

Circle what you saw OR write the number observed on top of the image.

What did you harvest?

Field Notes

_____

_____

_____

_____

_____

Date

Start/End Time

Location

Weather

Wind Speed

Wind Direction

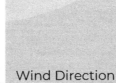

Shade the moon based on the phase.

Moon

Temperature

What are you hunting today?

Firearm/Gear

Hunting Companions

What did you see today?
Circle what you saw OR write the number observed on top of the image.

What did you harvest?

Field Notes

_____

_____

_____

_____

_____

Date

Start/End Time

Location

Weather

Wind Speed

Wind Direction

N

W   E

S

Shade the moon based on the phase.

Moon

Temperature

What are you hunting today?

Firearm/Gear

Hunting Companions

What did you see today?

Circle what you saw OR write the number observed on top of the image.

What did you harvest?

Field Notes

_____

_____

_____

_____

_____

Date

Start/End Time

Location

Weather

Wind Speed

Wind Direction

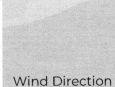

Shade the moon based on the phase.

Moon

Temperature

What are you hunting today?

Firearm/Gear

Hunting Companions

What did you see today?

Circle what you saw OR write the number observed on top of the image.

What did you harvest?

Field Notes

_____

_____

_____

_____

_____

Date

Start/End Time

Location

Weather

Wind Speed

Wind Direction

Shade the moon based on the phase.

Moon

Temperature

What are you hunting today?

Firearm/Gear

Hunting Companions

What did you see today?
Circle what you saw OR write the number observed on top of the image.

What did you harvest?

Field Notes

_____

_____

_____

_____

_____

Date

Start/End Time

Location

Weather

Wind Speed

Wind Direction

Shade the moon based on the phase.

Moon

Temperature

What are you hunting today?

Firearm/Gear

Hunting Companions

What did you see today?
Circle what you saw OR write the number observed on top of the image.

What did you harvest?

Field Notes

_____

_____

_____

_____

_____

Date

Start/End Time

Location

Weather

Wind Speed

Wind Direction

Shade the moon based on the phase.

Moon

Temperature

What are you hunting today?

Firearm/Gear

Hunting Companions

What did you see today?

Circle what you saw OR write the number observed on top of the image.

What did you harvest?

Field Notes

_____

_____

_____

_____

_____

Date

Start/End Time

Location

Weather

Wind Speed

Wind Direction

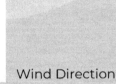

Shade the moon based on the phase.

Moon

Temperature

What are you hunting today?

Firearm/Gear

Hunting Companions

What did you see today?

Circle what you saw OR write the number observed on top of the image.

What did you harvest?

Field Notes

_____

_____

_____

_____

_____

Date

Start/End Time

Location

Weather

Wind Speed

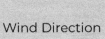

Wind Direction

Shade the moon based on the phase.

Moon

Temperature

What are you hunting today?

Firearm/Gear

Hunting Companions

What did you see today?

Circle what you saw OR write the number observed on top of the image.

What did you harvest?

Field Notes

_____

_____

_____

_____

_____

Date

Start/End Time

Location

Weather

Wind Speed

Wind Direction

Shade the moon based on the phase.

Moon

Temperature

What are you hunting today?

Firearm/Gear

Hunting Companions

What did you see today?
Circle what you saw OR write the number observed on top of the image.

What did you harvest?

Field Notes

_____

_____

_____

_____

_____

Date

Start/End Time

Location

Weather

Wind Speed

Wind Direction

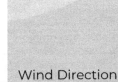

Shade the moon based on the phase.

Moon

Temperature

What are you hunting today?

Firearm/Gear

Hunting Companions

What did you see today?
Circle what you saw OR write the number observed on top of the image.

What did you harvest?

Field Notes

_____

_____

_____

_____

_____

Date

Start/End Time

Location

Weather

Wind Speed

Wind Direction

Shade the moon based on the phase.

Moon

Temperature

What are you hunting today?

Firearm/Gear

Hunting Companions

What did you see today?

Circle what you saw OR write the number observed on top of the image.

What did you harvest?

Field Notes

_____

_____

_____

_____

_____

Date

Start/End Time

Location

Weather

Wind Speed

Wind Direction

Shade the moon based on the phase.

Moon

Temperature

What are you hunting today?

Firearm/Gear

Hunting Companions

What did you see today?

Circle what you saw OR write the number observed on top of the image.

What did you harvest?

Field Notes

_____

_____

_____

_____

_____

Date

Start/End Time

Location

Weather

Wind Speed

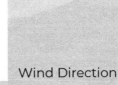

Wind Direction

Shade the moon based on the phase.

Moon

Temperature

What are you hunting today?

Firearm/Gear

Hunting Companions

What did you see today?

Circle what you saw OR write the number observed on top of the image.

What did you harvest?

Field Notes

_____

_____

_____

_____

_____

Date

Start/End Time

Location

Weather

Wind Speed

Wind Direction

*Shade the moon
based on the phase.*

Moon

Temperature

What are you hunting today?

Firearm/Gear

Hunting Companions

What did you see today?

Circle what you saw OR write the number observed on top of the image.

What did you harvest?

Field Notes

_____

_____

_____

_____

_____

Date

Start/End Time

Location

Weather

Wind Speed

Wind Direction

Shade the moon based on the phase.

Moon

Temperature

What are you hunting today?

Firearm/Gear

Hunting Companions

What did you see today?

Circle what you saw OR write the number observed on top of the image.

What did you harvest?

Field Notes

_____

_____

_____

_____

_____

Date

Start/End Time

Location

Weather

Wind Speed

Wind Direction

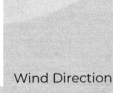

*Shade the moon
based on the phase.*

Moon

Temperature

What are you hunting today?

Firearm/Gear

Hunting Companions

What did you see today?

Circle what you saw OR write the number observed on top of the image.

What did you harvest?

Field Notes

_____

_____

_____

_____

_____

Date

Start/End Time

Location

Weather

Wind Speed

Wind Direction

Shade the moon based on the phase.

Moon

Temperature

What are you hunting today?

Firearm/Gear

Hunting Companions

What did you see today?
Circle what you saw OR write the number observed on top of the image.

What did you harvest?

Field Notes

_____

_____

_____

_____

_____

Date

Start/End Time

Location

Weather

Wind Speed

Wind Direction

Shade the moon based on the phase.

Moon

Temperature

What are you hunting today?

Firearm/Gear

Hunting Companions

What did you see today?

Circle what you saw OR write the number observed on top of the image.

What did you harvest?

Field Notes

_____

_____

_____

_____

_____

Date

Start/End Time

Location

Weather

Wind Speed

Wind Direction

Shade the moon based on the phase.

Moon

Temperature

What are you hunting today?

Firearm/Gear

Hunting Companions

What did you see today?

Circle what you saw OR write the number observed on top of the image.

What did you harvest?

Field Notes

_____

_____

_____

_____

_____

Date

Start/End Time

Location

Weather

Wind Speed

Wind Direction

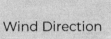

Shade the moon based on the phase.

Moon

Temperature

What are you hunting today?

Firearm/Gear

Hunting Companions

What did you see today?

Circle what you saw OR write the number observed on top of the image.

What did you harvest?

Field Notes

_____

_____

_____

_____

_____

Date

Start/End Time

Location

Weather

Wind Speed

Wind Direction

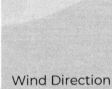

Shade the moon based on the phase.

Moon

Temperature

What are you hunting today?

Firearm/Gear

Hunting Companions

What did you see today?

Circle what you saw OR write the number observed on top of the image.

What did you harvest?

Field Notes

_____

_____

_____

_____

_____

EXPENSES

Date	Purchase	QTY	Unit Cost	Total Cost

EXPENSES

Date	Purchase	QTY	Unit Cost	Total Cost

Hunt Frequency

Goal:

Month	Number of Hunts

Hunt Frequency

Goal:

Month	Number of Hunts

Made in the USA
Las Vegas, NV
12 December 2024

13940186R00056